Questions and Answers About The United Methodist Church

Thomas S. McAnally

D1412312

Abingdon Press
Nashville

QUESTIONS AND ANSWERS ABOUT
THE UNITED METHODIST CHURCH

Copyright © 1995 by Abingdon Press

This book is printed on recycled, acid-free paper.

ISBN 0-687-01670-3

99 00 01 02 03 04 — 10 9 8 7

Layout and design by John Boegel

MANUFACTURED IN THE UNITED STATES OF AMERICA

Introduction

In the popular off-Broadway play *Sister Mary Ignatius Explains It All for You*, a nun uses flash cards to help a young parochial school student learn basics of the faith. She routinely flips through the cards, asking questions such as, "Who made you?" but stops abruptly when she comes to the question, "If God is all-powerful, why does He allow evil in the world?" With a furtive glance to the left and right, she quickly moves to the next card!

We're not trying to "explain it all for you" or to provide exhaustive, scholarly answers or encyclopedic definitions. Questions included are those often asked by church members and others interested in The United Methodist Church.

The assumption is that if a question is asked frequently by others, you may also have asked it—or wished you had. I have attempted to answer these questions with as much simplicity as possible. Admittedly the answers are incomplete.

If you want more detailed information, a list of basic resources is included at the close of this booklet. Also, you may wish to talk to your pastor or call InfoServ at 1-800-251-8140.

Baptism ushers you into the Christian church universal, the family of Christ. If you have not been baptized you will be asked to repent of your sins and profess your faith in God the Father, Jesus Christ, the Holy Spirit, and the Christian faith as contained in the scriptures of the Old and New Testaments. You will also be asked to promise to "keep God's holy will and commandments and walk in the same all the days of your life as a faithful member of Christ's holy church." **Your pastor may require that you participate in a membership class before being baptized or taking church membership vows.**

After baptism then what?

To be received into United Methodist membership you will be asked to be loyal to the church and "do all in your power to strengthen its ministries." Last, you will be received as a member of a particular congregation by committing yourself to "faithfully participate in its ministries by your prayers, your presence, your gifts, and your service."

What does the church teach about baptism?

Through baptism, we accept God's gift of grace through Jesus Christ and yield our lives to the leading of the Holy Spirit.

United Methodists baptize babies. Is it necessary for salvation?

When an infant is baptized, the parents promise to raise the child in a Christian home and the congregation recognizes its responsibility in the Christian nurture of the child. **Those vows are later reaffirmed by the child when he or she is confirmed as a church member.** While baptism is an important sacrament, it is not absolutely necessary for salvation. An infant who dies without having been baptized is as much within the love and care of God as the baptized infant.

How is baptism done in The United Methodist Church?

Sprinkling is most commonly used, but pouring and immersion are also permissible. To **sprinkle,** the pastor's hand is dipped into water and placed on the head of the person being baptized. For **immersion,** the person being baptized is completely dipped beneath water. The third option is simply to **pour water from a pitcher onto the head.** United Methodists are more concerned with the symbolism and meaning of the event than the exact form that might have been used in early times. **If the mode of baptism were essential to our Christian belief and practice, it is believed that the New Testament would be clear-cut in saying so.**

If I have already been baptized in another Christian denomination, must I be rebaptized to be a United Methodist?

No. Your previous baptism will be accepted, and you will only take vows of church membership.

What if I want to be baptized a second time?

Tradition of the church frowns upon rebaptism. Even when we drift from active involvement in the community of faith, we remain baptized. However, talk to your pastor about using a meaningful service for remembering and renewing your earlier baptism vows. The service can be found in *The United Methodist Hymnal* and *The United Methodist Book of Worship*.

What is the difference between baptism and confirmation?

One can be baptized any time after birth. Confirmation is the time when individuals confirm the vows that they took or that were taken by their parents at the time of baptism. Confirmation marks the time when a person is actually received as a member of The United Methodist Church. Generally, young people completing the sixth grade participate in a membership training class before they are confirmed.

A friend from another denomination half-jokingly said one can be a United Methodist and believe anything. Why does that impression exist among some people?

Probably because The United Methodist Church is not a creedal church that requires members to subscribe to a closely detailed system of beliefs. This does not mean, however, that United Methodists are not committed to basic Christian doctrines. Both the Articles of Religion and the Confession of Faith are embodied in our *Book of Discipline* as the doctrinal standards of the church. In addition, the *Standard Sermons* and *Notes upon the New Testament* from Methodism's founder, John Wesley, are included in the existing and established standards of doctrine and are accepted as landmark documents for United Methodists. We affirm core Christian doctrines such as: the Trinity—Father, Son, and Holy Spirit—both in personal experience and in the community of believers; salvation by grace through faith in Christ as Savior; the universal Church; the reign of God as both a present and future reality; the authority of Scripture in matters of faith; and the essential oneness of the Church in Jesus Christ. These are beliefs which we share with other denominations. We recognize the right of Christians to differ in doctrine, requiring only the essential belief that God is our Creator, that Jesus the Christ is our Lord and Savior, and that the Holy Spirit is ever present with us. "Our Theological Task," a twelve-page section of the *Book of Discipline,* encourages all United Methodists to reflect on God's gracious action in their lives. **While we acknowledge the primacy of Scripture in theological reflection, our attempts to grasp its meaning always involve the tradition of the church, personal experience, and the ability to reason for ourselves.**

You say the church is not creedal but I hear creeds recited at United Methodist worship services. Why?

While we have not made rigid acceptance of a creed the basis for uniting with the church's fellowship, we do not hesitate to use creeds in worship. They allow us to recall and affirm ancient and modern attempts to articulate the Christian tradition from a variety of perspectives. United Methodists believe that Scripture—"the primary source and criterion for Christian doctrine"—informed by tradition, experience, and reason, guides United Methodists in their development, evaluation, and understanding of Christian theology.

Why does the creed I often hear on Sunday morning affirm the catholic church?

The "holy catholic church," a phrase from the Apostles' Creed, indicates our belief that the church is essentially one, universal, and open to all. It is not a specific reference to the Roman Catholic Church.

What's different or distinctive about being a United Methodist?

There are no exclusively United Methodist doctrines. Although we have distinctive emphases, we have no affirmations that are not also believed by other Christian groups. United Methodists have traditionally proclaimed the following emphases:

- **the availability of God's grace for all;**
- **the essential unity of faith and works;**
- **salvation as personal and social;**
- **the church as a community of Christ's disciples who seek to share in God's mission;**
- **the inseparability of knowledge (intellect) and vital piety (devotion to religious duties and practices) as components of faith;**
- **seeking holiness of heart and life both as individuals and in our society;**
- **a cooperative ministry and mission in the world, often referred to as "connectionalism";**
- **the link between Christian doctrine and Christian living.**

How old is The United Methodist Church?

The present denomination was created in 1968 with the merger of The Methodist Church and The Evangelical United Brethren Church. The Evangelical United Brethren Church was the result of a 1946 union of the Church of the United Brethren in Christ and the Evangelical Church. The Methodist Church was the result of a 1939 union of the Methodist Episcopal Church, the Methodist Protestant Church, and the Methodist Episcopal Church, South.

John Wesley

Where did the church get its name?

John and **Charles Wesley** and a few other young men attending Oxford University met regularly in 1729 for intellectual and spiritual improvement and to help one another become better Christians. **So systematic were their habits of religious duty and their rules of conduct that other students referred to them as "Methodists."** The word "United" now in our name comes from The Evangelical United Brethren (EUB) Church, which united with The Methodist Church in 1968.

Charles Wesley

But aren't there other Methodist denominations?

Yes, several. The World Methodist Council, organized in 1881, is an association of 68 Methodist or united churches representing more than 29 million members and a constituency of 60 million in 108 countries of the world. The eight united churches in the Council are those in which Methodists have joined with others to form a new denomination such as the United Church of Canada.

How many Methodist denominations are there in the United States?

There are at least 19 Wesleyan denominations in the United States. Largest of these, with 8.7 million members, is The United Methodist Church. It ranks as the second largest Protestant denomination behind the Southern Baptists.

When did African Americans become part of Methodism?

Harry Hosier

From the early days of American Methodism. At the Christmas Conference of 1784 in Baltimore, persons in attendance included **Richard Allen** and **Harry Hosier,** both popular black preachers and former slaves. **Anne Sweitzer,** a slave, was on the roll of the first Methodist society in America, founded in Maryland in 1764. **A servant named Bettye helped start the John Street Church in New York, the first formal Methodist meetinghouse in America.** Two other black women contributed money to help build that chapel. Thousands of black Methodist converts, both slave and free, were worshiping among whites in camp meetings and revivals.

Isn't there an African American Methodist denomination?

There are several. The **African Methodist Episcopal Church,** formally organized in 1816, traces its origin to an incident at St. George's Methodist Episcopal Church in Philadelphia in 1787 when a group of African Americans left the church to protest racial discrimination. The **African Methodist Episcopal Zion Church** dates from 1796, when it was organized by a group of members protesting discrimination in the John Street Methodist Church in New York City. Their first church, named Zion, was built in 1800, and that word was later made part of the denominational title. The **Christian Methodist Episcopal Church** was established in 1870, after an agreement between white and black members of the Methodist Episcopal Church, South. These three historically black denominations have a combined membership of more than 4.5 million. An official committee representing these three black churches and The United Methodist Church is currently exploring the possibility of union.

Are there many African American members in The United Methodist Church today?

African Americans represent the largest ethnic minority membership in United Methodism today in the United States with about 300,000 members.

I thought the word *United* in our church's title had something to do with uniting black and white Methodists.

The title of The United Methodist Church was chosen in 1968 to reflect both The Methodist Church and The Evangelical United Brethren Church.

In order for three branches of Methodism to unite in 1939 it was considered politically necessary to create in the United States a jurisdiction for African Americans separate from five geographic jurisdictions. The terms of the later 1968 union required that all vestiges of this Central Jurisdiction be eliminated.

What about the number of members from other ethnic minority groups in the United States?

While exact statistics are not available, it is estimated that within United Methodism there are 50,000 Asian Americans, 40,000 Hispanic Americans, and 17,500 Native Americans.

What is the most serious problem in The United Methodist Church?

Ask a dozen people, and you would probably get a dozen different answers. Many church leaders contend we are having an "identity crisis" as a church. "We don't know who we are as a church and we have lost our sense of mission," recently observed Bishop Kenneth Carder of the Nashville (Tennessee) Area. He recommends that laity and clergy refocus on theology: "who God is, what God is doing, and what we are to be and do in response." He also suggests a recovery of a Wesleyan emphasis on obedience as a necessary component of faith in Christ. Of concern to many is the decline of membership in The United Methodist Church and other "mainline" denominations in the United States. There is no wide agreement on the cause of this decline.

How much has church membership declined?

Church membership peaked at 11 million in the two predecessor denominations of The United Methodist Church (Methodist and Evangelical United Brethren) in 1965. We have had a steady decline since that time, dropping to about 8.5 million members in the United States. However, United Methodist membership has grown outside the United States to more than 1 million members. Rapid growth is being recorded in the Philippines and parts of Africa. The fastest growth in the United States is among Korean immigrants. More members transfer into The United Methodist Church each year from other denominations than transfer out. Our most serious area of membership decline seems to be in the number of new Christians we receive by "profession of faith." Average attendance at the principal weekly worship service(s) has declined about a half million persons since The United Methodist Church was created in 1968.

What's the largest congregation in the denomination?

First United Methodist Church in Houston, with a membership of more than 13,500, followed by four other congregations, all in Texas: Highland Park, Dallas; First, Fort Worth; Memorial Drive, Houston; and St. Luke's, Houston. Seventy-three churches in the United States have more than 3,000 members, representing 0.2 percent of the churches and 3.8 percent of the membership. More than 66 percent of all United Methodist churches have fewer than 200 members, representing 22.9 percent of the denomination's total membership, 29.6 percent of worship attendance, and 31.7 percent of Sunday school attendance. (The 55,000-member Kwang Lim Methodist Church in Seoul, Korea, the largest congregation in the worldwide Methodist family, is not part of The United Methodist Church.)

The names of colleges and universities
such as Southern Methodist University and
Nebraska Wesleyan suggest they are related to
The United Methodist Church.
What is the relationship, if any?

One of the first actions taken by American Methodists when they organized in 1784 was to create Cokesbury College in Abingdon, Maryland. Since that time The United Methodist Church and its predecessor denominations have been affiliated in some way with 1,200 educational institutions. Today, 122 institutions have widely varying relationships to the denomination. These include 13 schools of theology; one medical college; 87 senior colleges and universities; 12 two-year colleges; and 9 college preparatory schools. The schools of theology receive support from the denomination-wide Ministerial Education Fund, and 11 historically black colleges receive support from the denomination-wide Black College Fund. There is no single pattern of church relationship. Southern Methodist University, for example, is legally owned by the eight-state South Central Jurisdiction, while the relationship with Boston University is more historic than legal. Some schools receive major financial assistance from a unit of the church or the entire denomination, while others receive little or no direct financial aid. **One of the most exciting projects in the church today is Africa University, the first United Methodist institution of higher**

education on the continent. United Methodists worldwide are raising money to build and operate the school, located in Zimbabwe.

Logo for Africa University

What about hospitals and retirement homes?

Again, their relationship to the church varies. Some are owned and operated by an annual conference. Others are independent of the conference, but reserve a number of positions on their governing boards for representatives of the church. A few institutions are owned by churchwide agencies. Some just have a historical relationship. Institutions with a relationship to the church include 58 hospitals; 135 retirement and long-term care facilities; 60 children, youth, and family service organizations; and 100 community centers.

Do lay people have much to say about what happens in the church?

In early days of American Methodism, clergy made most decisions for the church. **Today laity and clergy have equal voice in annual, jurisdictional, and general conferences of the church. There are also guidelines that encourage fair representation of women, young adults, and youth in decision making.** Of course, at the local level, lay persons are deeply involved in every aspect of the church's mission and ministry.

How are official positions on social matters determined by the church?

Only the General Conference—a representative body of no more than 1,000 clergy and lay persons which meets every four years—officially determines church policy and speaks on social issues. Through a set of Social Principles, the General Conference speaks to human issues from a biblical and theological foundation. These principles are intended to be instructive and persuasive. Agreement is not required, but members are called to a "prayerful, studied dialogue of faith and practice." Official resources of the church such as curriculum must reflect the official positions of the church.

What if I want to change a position of the church with which I disagree?

Each United Methodist has the right to petition General Conference. **Your pastor can assist you.** Every petition is considered, although similar petitions are usually grouped together. **You may also contact delegates from your annual conference to the General Conference.** These individuals are elected at the annual conference sessions in the year preceding the General Conference.

What is the church's stand on homosexuality?

The church affirms the sacred worth of homosexual persons, who like others, need the ministry and guidance of the church. **However, the church does not condone the practice of homosexuality and considers it "incompatible with Christian Teaching."** The church affirms that human and civil rights are due all persons. However, "self-avowed practicing" homosexuals are barred from ordination or appointment as clergy. No churchwide funds can be given to any gay caucus or group or used to "promote" the acceptance of homosexuality. Ceremonies that celebrate homosexual unions shall not be conducted by clergy and shall not be conducted in United Methodist churches.

What is the church's stand on abortion?

The church affirms the sanctity of unborn life. It also respects the mother who could suffer devastating damage from an unacceptable pregnancy. The church rejects abortion as a means of birth control, but when "life conflicts with life," the church supports the legal option of abortion after prayerful consideration by all parties involved.

What is the church's stand on divorce?

The church recognizes divorce as regrettable, but endorses the right of divorced persons to remarry.

What is the church's position on capital punishment?

The church opposes capital punishment and urges its elimination from all criminal codes.

How is The United Methodist Church organized?

The denomination is a democratic and representative organization. The manner by which the church is organized, the selection of leaders, and the way it uses its resources are determined by a majority of voting members at local, regional, and international meetings called "conferences."

What is a "charge conference"?

A charge includes one or more local churches. The charge conference—composed of all members of the Administrative Board or Administrative Council—meets at least once a year. The district superintendent usually presides. The charge conference is the connecting link between the local church and the annual conference and the larger church. A "church conference," where all church members participate and vote, may be authorized by the district superintendent.

What is a district superintendent?

An ordained clergyperson appointed by a bishop to supervise a region of about 50 churches. These regions vary greatly in geographic area.

What is an "annual conference"?

The annual conference is the basic body in the church. The term is a bit confusing because it refers both to a regional unit and to the meetings held by those regional units each year. **There are 68 annual (regional) conferences in the United States. Each year an equal number of lay members from local churches and the ordained clergy gather for annual conference sessions to approve, among other things, program and budget, and to speak to social concerns.** Every four years this body elects delegates to jurisdictional and General Conferences.

What is a "jurisdictional conference"?

A conference held in each of five geographic jurisdictions in the United States every four years. Primary functions of the jurisdictional conferences are to elect and assign bishops, determine the boundaries for episcopal areas, and implement General Conference legislation.

What is a "central conference"?

Central conferences, composed of United Methodist congregations in Africa, Europe, and the Philippines, function in much the same way as the U.S. jurisdictional conferences.

What is "General Conference"?

This international body of no more than 1,000 lay and clergy delegates meets every four years and is the only group that can make official policy for The United Methodist Church. Its decisions are included in *The Book of Discipline* and *The Book of Resolutions*.

How are General Conference delegates elected?

Every four years, members of the annual conference elect delegates to General Conference. Each annual conference is informed of the number of clergy and lay delegates to be elected, based on a formula determined by the number of full ministerial members and the number of local church members in that conference. Clergy vote for clergy; laypersons for laypersons. Annual conference members are given a blank sheet of paper on which they write the names of a given number of people to be elected. **Once an individual receives more than 50 percent of the votes, he or she becomes a delegate to the General Conference.**

What happens to the money I put in the collection plate?

Of every dollar contributed, about 80 cents is used in the local church; 15 cents for jurisdictional, area, annual conference and district work; 3 cents for general apportioned funds such as World Service; 1 cent for other general funds such as Advance Specials; and 1 cent for United Methodist Women. The local church expenditures each year total more than $3 billion.

What is a bishop?

A bishop is an ordained elder, elected by the jurisdictional or central conference, to serve in one of the top offices of the church. In the United States a bishop is elected for life. He or she is considered a general superintendent of the entire church but is assigned to four-year terms to oversee the work of the church in a particular area. The normal tenure in one area is eight years; the limit is twelve. A bishop must retire before reaching age 70.

How are bishops paid?

All U.S. bishops receive the same salary amount, according to a formula determined by the General Conference. In addition to salary, each bishop is provided an episcopal residence owned by the annual conference. Bishops in central conferences outside the United States are paid according to the pay scales in the economies of their respective regions.

How are pastors appointed?

A ll ordained clergy members of an annual conference (whether they serve as pastors of congregations or in other types of ministry) are appointed
annually by a bishop after consultation with district
superintendents, who consult closely with the local
church Pastor-Parish (or Staff Parish) Relations Committee. Committee members, representing the congregation, advise the superintendent whether they want
their pastor returned or whether a change in pastoral
leadership is desired. The bishop has final authority in
appointment making.

What is meant by "itinerant" clergy or the "itineracy"?

H istorically, Methodism has had an "itinerant"
clergy, meaning that all clergypersons of the
annual conference are subject to annual appointment
by a bishop. Being part of the itineracy means that a
clergyperson is willing to go where sent. This system
assures every pastor a church and every church a pastor. It also matches the gifts and graces of an individual with the needs of a particular church or area of service.

How long does a pas-tor stay with one church?

R ecent surveys indi-
cate that the mean
tenure of a pastor is
about four years.

How are pastors paid?

L ocal churches deter-
mine the amount of
the pastor's salary. Each
annual conference sets a
minimum salary, which it
subsidizes if the local congregation cannot afford to
pay it in full.

Are clergy ever fired?

Clergy may voluntarily "locate"—choose to step outside the regular itinerant or appointive system—or may be forcibly removed by "involuntary location." Ministerial credentials may be taken from a clergyperson if he or she is found guilty of charges which are clearly spelled out in the church's *Book of Discipline*. Sometimes such credentials are voluntarily surrendered.

In our large congregation we have several ministers—some are deacons and some are elders. What's the difference?

The man or woman appointed by the bishop as pastor of a local church is usually an ordained elder. Deacons and elders are both ordained, but the focus of their ministry is somewhat different. Deacons equip others for the church's ministry of service through teaching, proclamation, worship, and assisting elders as they administer the sacraments. Elders preach, teach the Word of God, administer the sacraments, order the church for its mission and service, and administer the *Discipline* of the church. Deacons and elders in full connection with an annual conference are appointed annually, but deacons are not guaranteed a place of employment in the church.

How can I become an ordained minister?

First, talk with your pastor about your interest or sense of God's call to full-time ministry. Your pastor can guide you through a process that begins with an application for candidacy. You must be a United Methodist and approved by your local church and a district and conference board of ordained ministry. Normally, you must complete four years of college and three years of study at an approved school of theology. There are other routes into the ordained ministry that you can discuss with your pastor.

How long have United Methodists had women pastors?

Women were ordained in some predecessor denominations of The United Methodist Church in the late 1800s but were not given equal rights with their male colleagues until 1956 in The Methodist Church. Today women are members of the annual conferences and as such are fully eligible for appointment as pastors, district superintendents, special appointments beyond the local church, or for election as bishops.

I've heard that our pastor is not really a member of our congregation. Is that true?

United Methodist clergy are members of the annual conference, the body to which they are amenable in the performance of their duties. They are not members of the local church.

Can lay people help the pastor serve the bread and grape juice during the Lord's Supper?

The United Methodist Church recognizes only baptism and the Lord's Supper as sacraments because they were the only acts ordained by Christ. Other events such as confirmation, marriage, and funeral services are obviously significant and important, but they are not considered sacraments. Yes. Lay members may also be trained to immediately deliver the consecrated communion elements to members confined at home, in a nursing home, or in a hospital.

Why does the church use grape juice in Communion?

Although the historic and ecumenical Christian practice has been to use wine, the use of unfermented grape juice by The United Methodist Church and its predecessors since the late nineteenth century expresses pastoral concern for recovering alcoholics, enables the participation of children and youth, and supports the church's witness of abstinence from alcoholic beverages.

Are children permitted to participate in the Lord's Supper?

Yes. The Lord's Supper—also referred to as Communion or Eucharist—is open to all persons. You do not have to be a member of the church to participate. Children may not fully comprehend what is going on, but they know when they are excluded.

Is anybody excluded from participating in the Lord's Supper?

Anyone may participate who responds affirmatively to the invitation: "Christ our Lord invites to his table all who love him, who earnestly repent of their sin and seek to live in peace with one another."

In the Communion service, what is meant by the "body and blood of Christ"?

The bread and wine represent the body and blood of Jesus as he spoke of them at the last supper with his disciples before being crucified. We do not believe that the elements literally turn into the body and blood of Christ.

Where can I find the basic positions and regulations of The United Methodist Church?

Two books will be most helpful: *The Book of Discipline*, and *The Book of Resolutions*. Both are produced every four years following General Conference sessions. The *Book of Discipline* is our manual of procedures and regulations. It covers every phase of church life: doctrine; guidance for Christian behavior; procedure and ritual for becoming a church member or a minister; details for organizing and administering local churches, districts, and conferences, as well as churchwide boards and agencies; rules of church law. The *Book of Resolutions* includes statements on social concerns approved by General Conference delegates.

How do United Methodists view other Christian bodies?

We strive for Christian unity and cooperation. The Constitution of The United Methodist Church declares that "the Lord of the Church is calling Christians everywhere to strive toward unity . . . through relationships with other Methodist churches and united churches . . . , through councils of churches, and through plans of union with churches of Methodist or other denominational traditions." The United Methodist Church is a member of the Consultation on Church Union, the National Council of the Churches of Christ in the U.S.A., the World Council of Churches, and the World Methodist Council.

Why are the colors changed on our Communion Table cloths and the stoles worn by our pastor and choir members?

The United Methodist Church and many other Christian bodies use color to mark important events in the life of the church. The church year begins with Advent, the four Sundays before Christmas Day. The color for Advent is purple. White is used from Christmas Day until Epiphany (January 6), marking the arrival of the wise men to see the infant Jesus. The color for the season from January 7 through Ash Wednesday is green, except for the first Sunday (the Baptism of Jesus) and the last Sunday before Ash Wednesday, which are white. The color for the preparation of Easter is purple (the forty days of Lent). Easter is white to celebrate the Resurrection. Pentecost (the fiftieth day after Easter) celebrates the coming of the Holy Spirit with red. Following Pentecost, the color for the season is green, except for the first and last Sundays and for All Saints Day; these days are white.

How can I get answers to questions not in this book?

Talk to your pastor or call InfoServ, the Church's nationwide, toll-free telephone service: 1-800-251-8140.

Suggested Reading

Allen, Charles L. *Meet the Methodists: An Introduction to The United Methodist Church.* Nashville: Abingdon Press, 1986.

The Book of Discipline, 1996. Nashville: The United Methodist Publishing House, 1992.

The Book of Resolutions, 1996. Nashville: The United Methodist Publishing House, 1992.

Carter, Kenneth L. *Sermons On United Methodist Beliefs.* Nashville: Abingdon Press, 1991.

Colaw, Emerson S. *Beliefs of a United Methodist Christmas,* 3rd edition, revised. Nashville: Discipleship Resources, 1994.

Custer, Chester E. *The United Methodist Primer,* revised edition. Nashville: Discipleship Resources, 1993.

Felton, Gayle. *By Water and the Spirit: Making Connections for Identity and Ministry.* Nashville: Discipleship Resources, 1997.

Frank, Thomas Edward. *Polity, Practice and the Mission of the United Methodist Church.* Nashville: Abingdon Press, 1997

*Hares, James C. *Essential Beliefs for United Methodists.* Nashville: Discipleship Resources, 1976.

Harmon, Nolan B. *Understanding the United Methodist Church,* revised edition. Nashville: Abingdon Press, 1974.

Historical Statement, in *The Book of Discipline of The United Methodist Church.* Nashville: The United Methodist Publishing House, 1992.

McElhenney, John G., editor. *United Methodism in America: A Compact History.* Nashville: Abingdon Press, 1992.

*Short, Roy H. *United Methodism in Theory and Practice.* Nashville: Abingdon Press, 1974.

*Stokes, Mack B. *Major United Methodist Beliefs.* Nashville: Abingdon Press, 1955, 1956, 1971.

*Stokes, Mack B. *Questions Asked by United Methodists.* Nashville: Discipleship Resources, 1979.

Thurston, Branson L. *The United Methodist Way,* revised. Nashville: Discipleship Resources, 1993.

Tuell, Jack M. *The Organization of The United Methodist Church,* revised. Nashville: Abingdon Press, 1993.

*Vernon, Walter N. *United Methodist Profile.* Nashville: Graded Press, 1959, 1968, 1972, 1983.

Waltz, Alan K. *Dictionary for United Methodists.* Nashville: Abingdon Press, 1991.

Washburn, Paul. *An Unfinished Church: A Brief History of the Union of The Evangelical United Brethren and The Methodist Church.* Nashville: Abingdon Press, 1984.

Yrigoyen, Charles Jr. and Warrick, Susan E. *Historical Dictionary of Methodism.* Lanham, Md., and London: The Scarecrow Press, Inc., 1996.

*No longer available for purchase. Check your local church library.

Questions and Answers
About
The United Methodist Church